Devotio Graduates

A 60-Day Devotional

Joanne Raines

Joanne Raines

Dedication

To all graduates embarking on new journeys, may this devotional be a beacon of hope, wisdom, and faith as you step into the future.

Table of Contents

A Message to Graduates

Dear Graduate,

Heartfelt congratulations on your remarkable achievement! This milestone marks an important chapter in your life, filled with joy, celebration, and exciting possibilities. Whether you're moving away, starting college, beginning a new job, or all three, this moment is a blend of anticipation and promise.

As you embark on this journey, I'd like to share some reflections that have guided me. Life brings various seasons, each with its own challenges and opportunities. Amidst these changes, one constant remains: the unwavering presence of Jesus Christ. Hebrews 13:8 reassures us, "Jesus Christ is the same yesterday, today, and forever." This truth offers comfort, reminding us that our Savior's love and guidance are ever-present.

In my experience, the closer my relationship with Jesus, the more peace and contentment I find. As you face new environments, people, and challenges, staying connected to him is vital. This book is a reminder to seek his guidance, rely on his hope, and find comfort in his presence.

Navigating life's transitions can be daunting, but remember you are never alone. Jesus illuminates your path and offers unwavering love and strength. Embrace this truth to anchor your soul in peace.

Cultivate a habit of faithful prayer and remain grounded in biblical truths. Prayer nurtures your relationship with God, providing solace and guidance. The Bible offers wisdom and encouragement, essential for facing life's decisions and challenges.

As you begin this new chapter, stay true to your values and keep your faith at the forefront. Surround yourself with supportive believers and seek mentors for guidance. Trust in God's perfect plan and timing.

May the Lord bless you abundantly and keep you close. Embrace your adventure with confidence, knowing Jesus is by your side, guiding you every step of the way.

Congratulations once again, and may this moment be the start of a life filled with purpose, joy, and the unwavering presence of our Savior.

Introduction: My Journey of Faith in Seattle

After graduating from the University of Washington in Seattle, I felt a mix of joy and anxiety. I was proud of my accomplishments, but I was also nervous about what lay ahead. With my degree in hand and dreams of making an impact in the tech industry, I moved into a small apartment downtown, ready to start my job at a bustling tech startup.

The first few weeks were both exciting and overwhelming. Navigating my new responsibilities, meeting deadlines, and adapting to a fast-paced environment was challenging. I often found myself questioning if I was truly prepared for this new chapter. One particularly stressful day, I remembered the devotional book my grandmother had given me at my graduation party. It had been sitting on my bedside table, untouched amidst the chaos of moving and starting my new job.

That evening, I decided to open the book and read the first devotion. The scripture passage was from Jeremiah 29:11, "For I know the plans I have for you, declares the Lord, plans for welfare and not for evil, to give you a future and a hope." The reflection spoke about trusting God's plan even when the path seemed unclear. It was exactly what I needed to hear. I felt a wave of peace wash over me, a reminder that I was not alone in this journey.

In the following weeks, I made it a habit to read a devotion every morning. Each day, I found messages that resonated with my experiences—whether it was dealing with self-doubt, learning to persevere, or expressing gratitude for small victories. These moments of reflection became my anchor, grounding me amidst the busyness of my new life.

On weekends, I explored Seattle, finding solace in the city's natural beauty. I hiked the trails of Discovery Park, kayaked on Lake Union, and visited the bustling Pike Place Market. These activities became my way of experiencing God's presence in nature and community. I also joined a local church group, where I met other young professionals who shared my faith and provided a supportive network.

One day, as I sat in my favorite coffee shop overlooking Puget Sound, I reflected on my journey since graduation. I realized how much I had grown—not just professionally, but spiritually. The devotional had been a constant companion, helping me navigate the ups and downs with faith and resilience.

My story is a testament to the power of faith during times of transition. As I continue my journey, I know that with God's guidance, I can face any challenge that comes my way. This devotional book had not only enriched my spiritual life but had also given me the courage to embrace the future with hope and confidence.

Day 1: Conquering Challenges

ROMANS 8:31 (NIV)

What, then, shall we say in response to these things? If God is for us, who can be against us?

Reflection

Jesus is by your side. When you align your actions with his intentions, nothing in the universe can obstruct you. Despite facing numerous challenges along the way, remain steadfast and never lose hope. With his assistance, you can conquer any hurdle. Understand that the path alongside him won't always be easy, but remember that He, your ever-present aid, holds boundless power.

Much of your stress stems from trying to force outcomes prematurely. Jesus exercises his authority chiefly through the timing of events. If you desire to walk closely with him and follow his lead, seek his guidance for each step forward. Rather than rushing towards your destination, let him determine the pace. Slow down, and savor the journey in his company.

Prayer

Dear Heavenly Father, Grant me the wisdom to align my actions with your intentions and the patience to trust in your perfect timing. Help me to savor the journey in your company, knowing that with your support, no obstacle can stand in my way. Amen.

Day 2: Reduce Your Burden

ISAIAH 41:10 (NIV)

So do not fear, for I am with you; do not be dismayed, for I am your God. I will strengthen you and help you; I will uphold you with my righteous right hand.

Reflection

The world can overwhelm you. Your mind gets caught up in a whirlwind of problems, twisting your thoughts into knots of anxiety. When you think like that, you push Jesus aside and your mind becomes clouded. Even though He wants to help, He won't force himself into your thoughts. He quietly waits in the background of your mind, hoping you'll remember that He's here with you.

When you shift your focus from your problems to his presence, your burdens suddenly feel lighter. The circumstances might not change, but you carry your load together. Your need to fix everything fades away as you connect deeply with him. Together, you can handle whatever today brings.

Prayer

Dear Lord, grant me strength to shift my focus from problems to your comforting presence. Help me find peace in knowing I'm not alone. Guide me to connect deeply with you, facing each challenge together. Amen.

Day 3: Each Day Is a Gift

PSALM 118:24 (NIV)

The Lord has done it this very day; let us rejoice today and be glad.

Reflection

Think of each day as an adventure, carefully planned out by your guide. Instead of trying to control the day according to your plans, pay attention to Jesus and what He has in store for you. Be grateful for this day, recognizing it as a precious gift. Trust that He is with you every moment, whether you feel his presence or not. A thankful, trusting attitude helps you see things from his perspective. A life lived close to him will never be boring or predictable.

Expect surprises every day! Instead of always looking for the easiest way, be willing to follow wherever He leads. No matter how difficult the path may seem, the safest place to be is by his side.

Prayer

Lord, help me trust your plans and be grateful for each day as a precious gift. Guide me to follow wherever you lead, knowing the safest place is by your side. Amen.

Day 4: Don't Be Afraid of Change

MATTHEW 28:5 (NIV)

The angel said to the women, 'Do not be afraid, for I know that you are looking for Jesus, who was crucified.

Reflection

Jesus is the risen one, shining upon you always. You worship a living deity, not some man-made idol. Your relationship with him is supposed to be dynamic and challenging as He permeates more and more areas of your life. Don't be afraid of change, for He is transforming you into a new creation, with old things passing away and new things always on the horizon. When you cling to old ways and resist change, you resist his work within you. He wants you to embrace everything He's doing in your life and find your security in him alone.

It's easy to idolize routine and find security in the boundaries you create, but every day presents unique circumstances. Don't try to fit today into the mold of yesterday. Instead, ask Jesus to open your eyes so you can see all the opportunities He has prepared for you in this precious day of life.

Prayer

Lord, help me embrace your transformative work in my life. Open my eyes to see the opportunities you have prepared for me today. Let me find my security in you alone and trust in your constant presence. Amen.

Day 5: Handle Your Freedom with Care

JOHN 15:5 (NIV)

*I am the vine; you are the branches. If you remain in
me and I in you, you will bear much fruit; apart from
me you can do nothing.*

Reflection

Make sure you rely on Jesus for everything you do.
Wanting to do things on your own, without him, usually
comes from being too proud. Being self-sufficient sneaks
into your thoughts and actions without you even
noticing. But without him, you can't really accomplish
anything important that lasts forever. What He wants
most for you is to learn to trust him in every situation.
He'll do whatever it takes to help you do this, but you
need to work with him too.

It would be easy for Jesus to teach you if He just took
away your free will or overwhelmed you with his power.
But He cares about you too much to take away the
amazing gift of free will He gave you as his image-bearer.
So, use your freedom wisely by always depending on
him. That way, you'll experience his presence and peace.

Prayer

Dear God, as I come before you today, I acknowledge my
need for your guidance and strength. Help me to be

versatile in my prayers, adapting them to the needs of each moment. Grant me the wisdom to trust in you completely, knowing that you are always with me. Amen.

Day 6: Take It Step by Step

PSALM 34:17–18 (NIV)

The righteous cry out, and the Lord hears them; he delivers them from all their troubles. The Lord is close to the brokenhearted and saves those who are crushed in spirit.

Reflection

You can live a victorious life by relying deeply on Jesus. People often think victory means always succeeding and never making mistakes. But those who succeed on their own tend to forget about him and go their own way. It's through problems, failures, weakness, and needing help that you learn to trust him. True dependence isn't just asking him to bless what you've already decided to do. It's coming to him with an open mind and heart, letting him plant his desires in you. He might give you a dream that seems impossible for you to achieve on your own. That's when your journey of depending on him deeply begins. It's a step-by-step journey of faith, leaning on him as much as you need to.

It's not a path of always succeeding but of facing many failures. However, each failure helps you grow, as you rely on him more and more. Enjoy the happiness of living a victorious life by trusting him more deeply.

Prayer

Lord, teach me to live a victorious life by relying deeply on you. Help me to understand that true dependence means opening my heart to your desires, even when they seem impossible. Guide me on this journey of faith, where failures lead to growth and greater reliance on you. May I find joy in trusting you more deeply each day. Amen.

Day 7: There's an Appropriate Time for Everything

ECCLESIASTES 3:1 (NIV)

There is a time for everything, and a season for every activity under the heavens.

Reflection

Stop trying to figure everything out before its time. Accept that you can only live one day at a time. When something comes up, ask Jesus if it's something you need to deal with today. If it's not, let it go and focus on what you need to do today. When you do this, your life will become beautifully simple: there's a time for everything, and everything happens at the right time. A life lived close to him isn't complicated or cluttered.

When you focus on being with him, many things that used to bother you won't bother you anymore. Even though the world can be messy and confusing, remember that He has overcome it all. He has told you these things so that you can have peace in him.

Prayer

Dear God, help me embrace the simplicity of living one day at a time, trusting in your perfect timing. Teach me to discern what needs my attention now and what can wait. As I focus on being with you, may I find peace amidst life's complexities. Thank you for overcoming the world and granting me serenity in your presence. Amen.

Day 8: Shut Off Distractions

PSALM 62:8 (NIV)

Trust in him at all times, you people; pour out your hearts to him, for God is our refuge.

Reflection

Listen to Jesus constantly. He has a lot to tell you, and there are many people and situations that need your prayers. He's teaching you to focus more and more on him, tuning out distractions with the help of his Spirit. Walk with him in trust, responding to what He's doing instead of trying to make everything fit your plans.

He died to set you free, and that includes freedom from constantly planning everything. When your mind is filled with a jumble of thoughts, you can't hear his voice. A mind consumed with planning worships the idol of control. Turn away from this idolatry and back to him. Listen to Jesus, and you'll live a full and abundant life!

Prayer

Heavenly father, grant me the grace to listen to you constantly, tuning out distractions with the guidance of your Spirit. Teach me to walk in trust, responding to your leading rather than my own plans. Free me from the idol of control and the constant need to plan everything. May I find fullness and abundance in listening to your voice. Amen.

Day 9: Approach the Day with Joy

PSALM 5:3 (NIV)

In the morning, Lord, you hear my voice; in the morning I lay my requests before you and wait expectantly.

Reflection

As you wake up in the morning, remember that Jesus is with you. Even if your thoughts are still foggy, He is clear-minded. Your early morning thoughts might be anxious until you connect with him. Invite him into your thoughts by whispering his name. Suddenly, your day will feel brighter and more manageable. You can't dread a day that is filled with his presence. Knowing that He is with you gives you confidence—you don't have to face anything alone.

Anxiety comes from asking the wrong question: "Can I handle what might happen?" The real question is not whether you can handle it on your own, but whether you and Jesus together can handle anything that comes your way. It's this partnership between you and him that gives you the courage to face the day with a smile.

Prayer

Heavenly Father, as the morning light breaks through, I awaken to your presence. Amidst the haze of early thoughts, you bring clarity and peace. Let me invite you into my day with a whispered prayer, infusing it with brightness and purpose. With you beside me, I face the day with confidence, knowing that together, we can navigate any challenge. Amen.

Day 10: Be on Guard

PSALM 89:15 (NIV)

Blessed are those who have learned to acclaim you, who walk in the light of your presence, Lord.

Reflection

Be careful not to fall into the trap of self-pity. When you're tired or unwell, it's the biggest danger you face. Don't even get close to the edge of that pit. The edges are fragile, and before you know it, you're falling in. It's much harder to climb out of the pit than to stay away from it. That's why Jesus warns you to be on your guard. There are a few ways to protect yourself from self-pity. When you focus on praising and thanking him, you can't feel sorry for yourself. And the closer you are to him, the farther away you are from the pit. Live in the light of his presence by keeping your eyes on him. Then you'll be able to endure whatever challenges come your way without stumbling or falling.

Prayer

Gracious Father, in moments of weariness or illness, guard my heart from the trap of self-pity. Let me not even approach its edge, for its grip is strong and its descent swift. Instead, help me to focus on praising and thanking you, drawing closer to your light. May the radiance of your presence illuminate my path, shielding me from the shadows of self-pity. With my eyes fixed on you, I trust that I can endure every challenge without stumbling. Amen.

Day 11: I'm Leading the Way

DEUTERONOMY 29:29 (NIV)

The secret things belong to the Lord our God, but the things revealed belong to us and to our children forever, that we may follow all the words of this law.

Reflection

I am guiding you through your life, step by step. Trust Jesus and let him lead you through today. The future may seem uncertain and fragile—that's normal. The unknown belongs to the Lord, and the future is part of that mystery. When you try to predict what's ahead, you're trying to take control of what is meant for him to handle. This act, like all worrying, is a form of rebellion because it doubts his promise to care for you.

Whenever you start to worry about what's to come, turn back to Jesus. He will show you the next step to take, and the one after that. Relax and enjoy your journey in his presence, trusting that He will clear the path for you as you move forward.

Prayer

Lord Jesus, as I journey through life, I place my trust in your guidance. In the face of uncertainty, I surrender to your wisdom, knowing that the future rests in your hands. When worries arise, draw me back to you, revealing the steps of my path one by one. In your presence, I find peace and assurance, trusting in your provision for each step of the journey ahead. Amen.

Day 12: Dealing with Uncertainty

MATTHEW 11:28 (NIV)

Come to me, all you who are weary and burdened, and I will give you rest.

Reflection

Take a moment to rest with Jesus. You've been traveling a tough, uphill path recently, and the future is unclear. Don't dwell on the past or worry about what's ahead. Instead, focus on him, your ever-present companion. Trust that He'll prepare you for whatever lies ahead on your journey.

He created time to protect you, so you wouldn't have to handle everything at once. Even though He's not limited by time, He connects with you in the present. Take this time to refresh yourself in his presence, breathing deeply. The greatest trust you can show is to enjoy each moment with him. He's here with you, watching over you wherever you go.

Prayer

Divine Companion, in the midst of life's challenges and uncertainties, I find solace in your presence. As I pause to rest with you, I release the burdens of the past and the worries of the future. Help me to focus on the present moment, knowing that you are with me always. May this time of refreshment in your presence renew my spirit and deepen my trust in you. Amen.

Day 13: Healing from Wounds

JAMES 4:2 (NIV)

You desire but do not have, so you kill. You covet but you cannot get what you want, so you quarrel and fight. You do not have because you do not ask God.

Reflection

I am a God who can mend what's broken. I can heal not just physical wounds but also mental pain, emotional hurt, shattered lives, and fractured relationships.

Just being near Jesus brings some level of healing. You naturally get some healing just by being close to him, whether you ask for it or not. But there's even more available if you ask. The first step to getting healing is to stay very close to him. This brings lots of benefits. As you get closer to him, He makes his will clearer to you.

When the time is right, He might nudge you to ask for healing, either for yourself or someone else. The healing might happen right away, or it might take time. That's up to him. Your job is to trust him completely and be thankful for the healing that's starting. He usually doesn't fix everything in a person's life. Even Paul, one of his followers, was told, "My grace is enough for you," when he asked for healing for something bothering him. But there's still a lot of healing available for those who are deeply connected to him. Ask, and you'll get it.

Prayer

Divine Healer, in your presence, brokenness finds restoration and wounds find healing. Help me draw close, trusting in your will and timing. Grant me wisdom to recognize your nudges and courage to ask for healing. Thank you for the restoration that begins in your presence. Amen.

Day 14: You're Recognized and Loved

Psalm 139:1–4 (NIV)

You have searched me, Lord, and you know me. You know when I sit and when I rise; you perceive my thoughts from afar. You discern my going out and my lying down; you are familiar with all my ways. Before a word is on my tongue you, Lord, know it completely.

Reflection

Come to Jesus when you need to understand yourself better. He knows you inside out, even better than you know yourself. He understands all the complexities of your life, and nothing about you is hidden from him. He looks at you with kindness, so don't worry about him knowing everything about you. Let the healing light of his presence shine into the deepest parts of you, cleansing, healing, refreshing, and renewing you. Trust him enough to accept his complete forgiveness, which He offers you all the time. This forgiveness, which cost him his life, is yours forever.

Forgiveness is at the very heart of his constant presence with you. He will never abandon you or leave you alone. When it feels like nobody else gets you, just come closer to him. Be happy in knowing that He understands you completely and loves you perfectly. As He fills you with his love, you become a source of love that overflows into the lives of others.

Prayer

Lord Jesus, in your presence, I find understanding and acceptance. Shine your healing light into the depths of my being. Help me trust in your forgiveness and assurance. Your constant presence assures me that I am never alone. Fill me with your love, that I may overflow with compassion toward others. Amen.

Day 15: Let Go of Your Errors

ROMANS 8:28 (NIV)

And we know that in all things God works for the good of those who love him, who have been called according to his purpose.

Reflection

Ease up on yourself. Jesus can turn even your mistakes into something good. Your mind often dwells on the past, wishing you could undo decisions you regret. But that just wastes time and makes you frustrated. Instead of getting stuck in the past, give your mistakes to him. Trust him and believe that his endless creativity can turn both good and bad choices into something beautiful. Because you're human, you'll keep making mistakes. Thinking you should never mess up is a sign of pride. Your failures can actually be a good thing, making you more humble and understanding towards others when they struggle. Most importantly, your mistakes show how much you need Jesus. He can turn the mess of your mistakes into something beautiful. Trust him and see what He can do.

Prayer

Heavenly Father, in times of self-doubt and regret, I release my mistakes to you. Grant me strength to trust in your creativity, bringing good from my errors. Help me embrace my humanity, learning from mistakes with humility and empathy. Remind me of my dependence on you, transforming my mess into beauty. Amen.

Day 16: Everything Is Mine

HEBREWS 12:28–29 (NIV)

Therefore, since we are receiving a kingdom that cannot be shaken, let us be thankful, and so worship God acceptably with reverence and awe, for our 'God is a consuming fire.

Reflection

Let Jesus show you how to be grateful. Start by recognizing that everything—every possession and every part of who you are—belongs to him. Each new day that begins is a gift from him, not something to just expect. The world is full of blessings from him, showing that He's always around.

If you slow down and take your time, you can find him in everything. Some of his dearest children have been stuck in beds due to sickness or locked away in prisons. Others have chosen to spend time alone with him, learning from it. The key to being thankful is to see everything from his point of view. his world is like your classroom, and his word guides you like a lamp on a dark path.

Prayer

Dear Father, help me to cultivate gratitude by recognizing that everything belongs to you. Each new day is a precious gift from your hand. Open my eyes to see your blessings all around me, even in challenging circumstances. Guide me to view life from your perspective, seeing every moment as an opportunity to learn and grow in your love. Amen.

Day 17: Pray Consistently

1 THESSALONIANS 5:17 (NIV)

Pray continually.

Reflection

I'm inviting you to live a life where you're always connected with Jesus. Part of your training involves learning to rise above whatever situation you're in, even when life gets chaotic. You might wish for a simpler life, where you can talk to him without any interruptions. But He wants you to let go of the idea of a perfect, tidy world. Embrace each day as it comes, and find him in the middle of it all.

Share every part of your day with him, including how you feel. Remember, your main aim isn't to control or fix everything around you; it's to keep talking with him. A successful day is one where you've stayed connected with him, even if you haven't finished everything on your to-do list. Don't let your to-do list become your main focus, whether it's written down or just in your head. Instead, ask his spirit to guide you moment by moment. He'll keep you close to him.

Prayer

Heavenly Father, guide me to live connected with you, rising above life's chaos. Help me embrace each day as it comes, finding you in every moment. Keep me focused on our connection rather than controlling everything. Amen.

Day 18: Choose Your Words Wisely

PROVERBS 12:18 (NIV)

The words of the reckless pierce like swords, but the tongue of the wise brings healing.

Reflection

Be careful with your words. They have immense power to either uplift or hurt. When you speak without thinking or speak negatively, you harm both yourself and others. The ability to speak is a remarkable gift, given only to those Jesus made in his image. You need guidance in using this power responsibly.

While the world may praise sharp comebacks, Jesus' advice on communication is different: Listen first, speak slowly, and don't rush to anger. Ask his spirit to assist you whenever you speak. You've learned to pray, "Help me, Holy Spirit," before picking up the phone, and you've seen the benefits of this practice. Apply the same approach to your interactions with others. If they're quiet, pray before speaking to them. If they're talking, pray before responding. These prayers may be quick, but they connect you with his presence. This way, your words are guided by his spirit. As you replace negative speech with positive patterns, you'll be surprised at how much joy increases in your life.

Prayer

Heavenly Father, guide my words to uplift rather than hurt. Grant me wisdom to speak slowly and listen first. Help me to invite your Spirit's guidance in every conversation. May my words reflect your love and bring joy to those around me. Amen.

Day 19: Evolve with Grace

COLOSSIANS 3:13 (NIV)

Bear with each other and forgive one another if any of you has a grievance against someone. Forgive as the Lord forgave you.

Reflection

Don't expect fairness in this life. People will say and do things that hurt you, even when you don't deserve it. When someone mistreats you, try to see it as a chance to grow in kindness. Aim to forgive quickly those who hurt you. Don't worry about proving yourself right. Instead of being consumed by what others think of you, focus on Jesus. In the end, it's his opinion of you that truly matters.

As you build your relationship with him, remember that He's clothed you in his righteousness and holiness. He sees you wearing these beautiful garments, which He bought for you with his own blood. This isn't fair either; it's a pure gift. When others treat you unfairly, remember that his ways are much better than fairness. his ways are filled with peace and love, which He's poured into your heart through his spirit.

Prayer

Lord Jesus, guide me to grow in kindness and quick forgiveness, focusing on your opinion of me. Remind me of the beautiful garments of righteousness and holiness you've given me. Though fairness may be lacking, your ways are filled with peace and love. Amen.

Day 20: Longing for Approval

Philippians 4:6–7 (NIV)

Do not be anxious about anything, but in every situation, by prayer and petition, with thanksgiving, present your requests to God. And the peace of God, which transcends all understanding, will guard your hearts and your minds in Christ Jesus.

Reflection

Come to Jesus and find peace. his presence surrounds you with a peace that goes beyond what you can understand. Instead of trying to solve everything on your own, you can rest in the company of someone who knows it all. When you rely on him with trust, you'll feel calm and whole. That's how He intended you to live: connected closely to him.

When you're with others, you often try to meet their expectations, whether real or imagined. You feel pressured to please them, and it becomes harder to sense his presence. Trying to win their approval drains you in the end. Instead of offering them the refreshing spirit within you, it's like giving them dry crumbs. But that's not the way He wants it to be for you! Stay connected with him, even in your busiest times. Let his spirit guide your words, as you bask in the peaceful light of his presence.

Prayer

Heavenly Father, help me to rely on you with trust, finding calm and wholeness. Guide me to stay connected with you, even amidst busyness. May your Spirit guide my words, as I bask in the peaceful light of your presence. Amen.

Day 21: Protect Your Mind

Psalm 112:7 (NIV)

They will have no fear of bad news; their hearts are steadfast, trusting in the Lord.

Reflection

Focus your worship solely on Jesus. Whatever occupies your mind the most becomes like your god. If you dwell on worries too much, they can turn into idols. Anxiety can take on a life of its own, spreading through your mind like a parasite. Break free from this trap by affirming your trust in him and finding renewal in his presence.

What happens in your mind is hidden from others, but He sees your thoughts all the time, looking for signs of trust in him. He's happy when your mind turns to him. Be careful with your thoughts; choosing good ones will keep you close to him.

Prayer

Lord Jesus, help me to focus my worship solely on you. Guide me to break free from the trap of worry and anxiety by affirming my trust in you and finding renewal in your presence. May my thoughts reflect trust and draw me closer to you. Amen.

Day 22: Devote Time to Me

Revelation 12:10 (NIV)

Then I heard a loud voice in heaven say: 'Now have come the salvation and the power and the kingdom of our God, and the authority of his Messiah. For the accuser of our brothers and sisters, who accuses them before our God day and night, has been hurled down.

Reflection

Spending time alone with Jesus is crucial for your well-being. It's not something you should feel guilty about; it's a necessity. Remember, Satan loves to accuse believers and make them feel guilty, especially when they're enjoying his presence. So, if you feel those accusing thoughts, it's likely a sign that you're doing something right.

Use your faith as a shield to protect yourself from these attacks. Talk to Jesus about what you're going through, and ask him to guide you. Stand firm against the devil, and he'll run away from you. Draw close to Jesus, and He'll draw close to you.

Prayer

Heavenly Father, guide me to prioritize spending time alone with you for my well-being. Protect me from feelings of guilt and accusation, using my faith as a shield. Help me to talk to you about what I'm going through and to stand firm against the devil's attacks. As I draw close to you, may you draw close to me. Amen.

Day 23: Have Faith in Me Regardless of Circumstances

Psalm 52:8 (NIV)

But I am like an olive tree flourishing in the house of God; I trust in God's unfailing love for ever and ever.

Reflection

Make an effort to trust Jesus more in every aspect of your life. Anything that makes you anxious is an opportunity for growth. Instead of avoiding these challenges, welcome them, eager to discover all the blessings He's hidden within the difficulties. If you truly believe that He's in control of every part of your life, you can trust him in every situation. Don't waste your energy regretting how things are or dwelling on what could have been. Start with the present moment—accepting things just as they are—and look for his guidance in those circumstances.

Trust is like a sturdy staff you can rely on as you journey uphill with Jesus. If you consistently put your trust in him, the staff will support you as much as you need. Lean on it, trust in him completely with all your heart and mind.

Prayer

Lord Jesus, help me to trust you more in every aspect of my life and to see challenges as opportunities for growth and blessings. Grant me the strength to rely on trust as a sturdy staff on my journey with you. Amen.

Day 24: Your Future Is Guaranteed

Psalm 37:23–24 (NIV)

The Lord makes firm the steps of the one who delights in him; though he may stumble, he will not fall, for the Lord upholds him with his hand.

Reflection

You belong to Jesus forever and beyond, into eternity. Nothing can take away your place in heaven. He wants you to understand just how secure you are! Even if you stumble along your journey in life, He'll never let go of your hand.

Knowing that your future is completely secure can set you free to live fully today. He's planned this day for you with great care and attention to detail. Instead of seeing the day as an empty page you need to fill, try living it in a responsive way, keeping an eye out for what He's doing. It might sound simple, but it requires a deep trust, knowing that his way is always perfect.

Prayer

Heavenly Father, remind me that I belong to you forever, secure in your love and care. Help me to trust in your plans for each day, living responsively to your guidance. May I find freedom in knowing that my future is secure in your hands. Amen.

Day 25: Wait with Hope

John 14:1 (NIV)

Do not let your hearts be troubled. You believe in God; believe also in me.

Reflection

Waiting, trusting, and hoping are closely linked, like golden threads woven together to form a strong chain. Trusting is at the core because it's the response Jesus desires most from his children. Waiting and hoping enhance the central trust and strengthen the connection between you and him.

When you wait for Jesus to act, keeping your focus on him, it shows genuine trust. If you say, "I trust you," but you're anxiously trying to control things, your words don't carry much weight. Hoping looks toward the future, linking you to your heavenly inheritance. But the benefits of hope are felt in the present. Because you belong to Jesus, waiting isn't just about passing time; you can wait with expectation, full of hopeful trust. Stay alert, keeping watch for even the faintest sign of his presence.

Prayer

Heavenly Father, help me to wait, trust, and hope in you, intertwining these golden threads into a strong chain of faith. May my trust in you be genuine, expressed through patient waiting and hopeful anticipation. Guide me to stay alert, keeping watch for signs of your presence. Amen.

Day 26: Equipped for Today

Psalm 84:12 (NIV)

Lord Almighty, blessed is the one who trusts in you.

Reflection

Trust Jesus one day at a time. This keeps you close to him, ready to follow his lead. Trust doesn't come naturally, especially for those who have been deeply hurt. his spirit inside you is like a teacher, helping you with this supernatural task. Listen to his gentle guidance; be open to his nudges.

Make a conscious choice to trust Jesus in every situation. Don't let your need to understand everything distract you from his presence. He'll give you what you need to face today with strength as you rely on him deeply. Tomorrow has its own worries; don't get caught up in them. Trust Jesus, one day at a time.

Prayer

Heavenly Father, guide me to trust you one day at a time, staying close to you and following your lead. Help me to listen to the gentle guidance of your Spirit within me, making a conscious choice to trust you in every situation. Grant me the strength to face today with confidence as I rely on you deeply. Amen.

Day 27: Let Go of Old Ways

Romans 8:38–39 (NIV)

For I am convinced that neither death nor life, neither angels nor demons, neither the present nor the future, nor any powers, neither height nor depth, nor anything else in all creation, will be able to separate us from the love of God that is in Christ Jesus our Lord.

Reflection

Come closer to Jesus with a heart full of gratitude, knowing that your life is overflowing with blessings. Gratitude helps you see him more clearly and rejoice in your loving relationship. Nothing can separate you from his love! That's what keeps you secure. Whenever you feel anxious, remind yourself that your security comes from him alone, and He is completely trustworthy.

You'll never have full control over your circumstances, but you can relax and trust that He's in control. Instead of chasing after a safe, predictable life, seek to know him more deeply and broadly. He wants to make your life an amazing adventure, but you have to let go of old ways. He's always doing something new in the lives of those He loves. Stay alert for all the wonderful things He has in store for you.

Prayer

Lord Jesus, fill my heart with gratitude, knowing my life overflows with blessings. Remind me nothing can separate me from your love. Grant me faith to trust in your unwavering trustworthiness. Guide me to embrace the adventure of knowing you more deeply. Amen.

Day 28: Everlasting Help

Psalm 46:1 (NIV)

God is our refuge and strength, an ever-present help in trouble.

Reflection

I softly make my presence known to you. Like gentle colors shimmering around you, I softly tap at the door of your awareness, seeking to be let in. Despite having all the power in heaven and on earth, I am infinitely tender with you. The weaker you feel, the more gently I approach you. Let your weakness be like a door through which I enter your life. Whenever you feel inadequate, remember that I am always here to help you.

Have hope in Jesus, and you'll be shielded from feelings of depression and self-pity. Hope is like a golden rope connecting you to heaven. The more you hold onto this rope, the more He takes on the weight of your burdens, making them lighter for you. Heaviness isn't part of his kingdom. Cling to hope, and his rays of light will reach you even in the darkest times.

Prayer

Heavenly Father, as gentle colors shimmer around me, remind me of your tender presence seeking to be let in. Grant me strength to see my weaknesses as opportunities for you to enter my life. Help me hold onto hope, connecting me to your light even in the darkest times. Amen.

Day 29: The Ultimate Safe Haven

LUKE 1:37 (NIV)

For no word from God will ever fail.

Reflection

Come to Jesus with all your weaknesses: physical, emotional, and spiritual. Find comfort in his presence, knowing that nothing is impossible for him. Shift your focus away from your problems and fix your attention on him. Remember that He can do far more than you could ever ask or imagine. Instead of trying to tell him what to do, try to tune in to what He's already doing.

When anxiety tries to creep into your thoughts, remind yourself that Jesus is your shepherd. Ultimately, He's taking care of you, so there's no need to be afraid of anything. Instead of trying to control your life, surrender yourself to his will. Even if it feels scary or risky, the safest place to be is within his will.

Prayer

Heavenly Father, in my weaknesses, I find comfort in your presence, knowing nothing is impossible for you. Help me shift my focus to your power and surrender to your will, finding safety and peace. Amen.

Day 30: Cheer Up and Laugh

Philippians 4:13 (NIV)

I can do all this through him who gives me strength.

Reflection

It's good that you recognize your weakness. It keeps you turning to Jesus, your strength. Abundant life isn't about health and wealth; it's about living in constant reliance on him. Instead of trying to force the day into your plans, relax and watch for what He's doing. This mindset will help you enjoy him and discover what He has in store for you. It's much better than struggling to make things go your way.

Don't take yourself too seriously. Lighten up and share a laugh with Jesus. With him on your side, what do you have to worry about? He can equip you to handle anything, as long as it's within his will. The tougher your day, the more He longs to assist you. Anxiety traps you in your own thoughts, but when you look to him and say his name, you break free and receive his help. Focus on Jesus, and you'll find peace in his presence.

Prayer

Dear Lord, help me to embrace my weaknesses and rely on your strength. Teach me to relax and look for your guidance rather than forcing my plans. Lighten my heart and remind me to find joy in your presence. Free me from anxiety, and let me find peace by focusing on you. Amen.

Day 31: Love Abundantly

JAMES 4:7–8 (NIV)

Submit yourselves, then, to God. Resist the devil, and he will flee from you. Come near to God and he will come near to you. Wash your hands, you sinners, and purify your hearts, you double-minded.

Reflection

Open your mind and heart—your entire being—to fully receive Jesus' love. Many of his children go through life feeling starved for love because they haven't learned how to receive it. Receiving love is an act of faith: believing that Jesus loves you with boundless, everlasting love. It's also a discipline: training your mind to trust him and approaching him with confidence.

Remember, the evil one is the father of lies. Learn to recognize his deceptive thoughts. One of his favorite tricks is to make you doubt Jesus' unconditional love. Don't let these lies go unchallenged! Resist the devil in Jesus' name, and he will retreat from you. Draw near to Jesus, and his presence will surround you with love.

Prayer

Heavenly Father, help me open my mind and heart to fully receive your boundless love. Strengthen my faith to trust in your everlasting love and to recognize and resist the lies of the evil one. Draw me near, and surround me with your comforting presence. Amen.

Day 32: Yearning for Greater Things

Philippians 4:19 (NIV)

And my God will meet all your needs according to the riches of his glory in Christ Jesus.

Reflection

Your needs and Jesus' abundance are a perfect match. He never intended for you to be self-sufficient. Instead, He created you to rely on him, not just for your daily needs, but also to fulfill your deepest longings. He carefully crafted your desires and feelings of incompleteness to lead you to him. So, don't try to bury or ignore these feelings.

Be cautious of trying to satisfy these longings with temporary things like people, possessions, or power. Come to Jesus with all your needs, with your defenses down, and a desire to be blessed. As you spend time in his presence, your deepest longings will be satisfied. Embrace your neediness, as it allows you to find true fulfillment in him.

Prayer

Heavenly Father, help me to recognize that my needs align perfectly with your abundance. Teach me to rely on you for all my needs and deepest longings, rather than seeking temporary satisfaction elsewhere. Guide me to come to you with openness and a desire to be blessed, finding true fulfillment in your presence. Amen.

Day 33: Acknowledge My Timing

Psalm 36:9 (NIV)

For with you is the fountain of life; in your light we see light.

Reflection

I'm actively working on your behalf. Bring Jesus all your concerns, even your dreams. Talk to him about everything, letting his presence shine light on your hopes and plans. Spend time allowing his light to breathe life into your dreams, gradually turning them into reality. This is a practical way of working together with Jesus. He, the creator of the universe, has chosen to collaborate with you in creating.

Don't rush this process. If you want to work with Jesus, you have to accept his timeline. Rushing isn't his style. Just like Abraham and Sarah had to wait many years for the fulfillment of God's promise—a son—how much more they cherished him because of their long wait! Remember, faith is the assurance of things hoped for, believing in the reality of what isn't yet seen.

Prayer

Heavenly Father, I bring you all my concerns and dreams, knowing that you actively work on my behalf. Help me to talk to you about everything, allowing your presence to illuminate my hopes and plans. Guide me to collaborate with you in creating, trusting in your timeline. May I have faith in the fulfillment of my hopes, even when they are yet unseen. Amen.

Day 34: I Am Worth the Risk

PSALM 23:4 (NIV)

Even though I walk through the darkest valley, I will fear no evil, for you are with me; your rod and your staff, they comfort me.

Reflection

Be ready to take risks with Jesus. If that's where He's guiding you, it's the safest place to be. Your desire for a risk-free life is a form of disbelief. Your longing to stay close to Jesus contradicts your efforts to avoid risk. You're approaching a crucial point in your journey. To follow Jesus wholeheartedly, you need to let go of your tendency to play it safe.

Let Jesus guide you step by step through today. If your main focus is on him, you can walk through dangerous paths without fear. Eventually, you'll learn to relax and enjoy the adventure of your journey together. As long as you stay close to Jesus, his sovereign presence will protect you wherever you go.

Prayer

Lord Jesus, guide me to embrace risks when they align with your guidance, knowing it's the safest place to be. Grant me courage to follow you wholeheartedly, focusing on your presence as I walk without fear. Amen.

Day 35: Spend Your Time Wisely

Romans 12:2 (NIV)

Do not conform to the pattern of this world, but be transformed by the renewing of your mind. Then you will be able to test and approve what God's will is—his good, pleasing and perfect will.

Reflection

Relax in my healing, holy presence. Allow me to transform you during this time alone with me. As you focus more on me, trust will replace fear and worry. Your mind is like a seesaw: as your trust in me rises, fear and worry decline. Spending time with me not only strengthens your trust but also helps you discern what truly matters.

Energy and time are valuable and limited resources, so you need to use them wisely by focusing on what is important. As you walk closely with me and immerse your mind in Scripture, I will guide you on how to spend your time and energy. My Word is a lamp to your feet; my presence is a light for your path.

Prayer

Dear Lord, help me to relax in your healing presence and be transformed. As I focus on you, let trust replace fear and worry. Guide me to use my time and energy wisely, discerning what truly matters. Let your Word light my path and your presence lead me. Amen.

Day 36: Opportunities to Learn

Isaiah 30:20–21 (NIV)

Although the Lord gives you the bread of adversity and the water of affliction, your teachers will be hidden no more; with your own eyes you will see them. Whether you turn to the right or to the left, your ears will hear a voice behind you, saying, 'This is the way; walk in it.

Reflection

When you encounter a problem that seems insurmountable, view it as an opportunity for growth. Think of it as having a personal tutor guiding you through a lesson in life. The more open you are to learning, the more wisdom you can gain from the experience. Approach the challenge with faith and gratitude, recognizing it as a chance for growth. Seek assistance in understanding the lessons embedded within the difficulty. By shifting your perspective and appreciating the problem, you prevent it from weighing you down. Instead, your gratitude elevates you, transforming the problem into a stepping stone toward lasting rewards.

Prayer

Dear Lord, grant me wisdom to see challenges as opportunities for growth. Help me understand their lessons and guide me through them. Amen.

Day 37: Put Your Trust in Me

MATTHEW 6:34 (NIV)

Therefore do not worry about tomorrow, for tomorrow will worry about itself. Each day has enough trouble of its own.

Reflection

Trust that what's ahead won't overwhelm you! It's not just a suggestion; it's a command. Time's broken into days and nights so you can handle life bit by bit. God's grace is enough, but it's meant for today. When you fret about tomorrow, you pile up burdens you shouldn't carry. Release that weight by trusting fully. Anxious thoughts may swarm, but trust brings you to God's presence. Reaffirm your faith, and worry fades. Keep trusting, keep enjoying God's presence.

Prayer

Heavenly Father, grant me the wisdom to learn from my challenges. Help me appreciate them as opportunities for growth. Guide me to understand the lessons they offer, and let gratitude lift me above them. May these obstacles lead to lasting benefits. Amen.

Day 38: Absence of Resentment

1 Peter 5:6 (NIV)

Humble yourselves, therefore, under God's mighty hand, that he may lift you up in due time.

Reflection

To consistently live in Jesus's presence, you need to address and overcome your rebellious tendencies. When something disrupts your plans or desires, you tend to resent it. Try to notice each instance of resentment, no matter how small it may seem. Don't suppress those feelings; let them come to the surface so you can deal with them. Ask the Spirit to help you become more aware of resentful feelings. Bring them boldly into Jesus's presence so He can free you from them.

The ultimate solution to rebellious tendencies is submitting to his authority over you. You might intellectually acknowledge his sovereignty, which makes the world less scary. But when his will interferes with your control, you often react with resentment. The best response to loss or disappointment is praise: "The Lord gives and the Lord takes away. Blessed be the name of the Lord." Remember that all good things—your possessions, family, health, abilities, time—are gifts from him. Instead of feeling entitled to these blessings, respond with gratitude. Be ready to let go of anything He takes from you, but never let go of his hand.

Prayer

Dear Lord, help me overcome my rebellious tendencies and submit to your authority. Make me aware of any resentment within me, and guide me to bring it into your presence for freedom. Teach me to praise you in all circumstances and to be grateful for your gifts. Hold my hand, Lord, as I navigate loss and disappointment. Amen.

Day 39: Treasure Every Blessing

Matthew 1:23 (NIV)

The virgin will conceive and give birth to a son, and they will call him Immanuel" (which means "God with us).

Reflection

Try to enjoy life more. Relax and remember that Jesus is with you. He made you with a big capacity to know him and enjoy his presence. It displeases him when his people go through life with sour faces and rigid attitudes. But when you approach each day with childlike delight, savoring every blessing, you show your trust in him, your constant shepherd.

The more you focus on his presence with you, the more you can truly enjoy life. Glorify him by finding pleasure in him. That's how you show the world that Jesus is with you.

Prayer

Dear Lord, grant me the ability to find joy in life and to relax in your presence. Thank you for allowing me to know and enjoy you. Help me approach each day with childlike delight, cherishing your blessings. May my happiness glorify you and reveal your presence to the world. Amen.

Day 40: A Better Path Ahead

1 CORINTHIANS 10:10 (NIV)

*And do not grumble, as some of them did—and were
killed by the destroying angel.*

Reflection

Let Jesus guide you through this day. There are many
paths you could take from morning to night. Stay alert
to the choices you make along the way, always aware of
Jesus's presence. You'll make it through this day one way
or another. One way is to grumble and stumble, dragging
your feet. Eventually, you'll reach the end of the day, but
there's a better way.

You can choose to walk with Jesus on the path of peace,
leaning on him as much as you need. There will still be
challenges, but you can face them confidently with his
strength. Thank him for each problem you encounter,
and see how He turns trials into blessings.

Prayer

Heavenly Father, guide me through this day. Help me
stay alert to the choices I make, always aware of your
presence. I can stumble and grumble or walk with you
on the path of peace. Give me strength to face challenges
confidently and turn trials into blessings. Amen.

Day 41: When Things Don't Go as Planned

1 Peter 5:5–6 (NIV)

In the same way, you who are younger, submit yourselves to your elders. All of you, clothe yourselves with humility toward one another, because, 'God opposes the proud but shows favor to the humble.' Humble yourselves, therefore, under God's mighty hand, that he may lift you up in due time.

Reflection

When things don't go your way, accept the situation right away. If you dwell on feelings of regret, they can easily turn into resentment. Remember that Jesus is in control of your circumstances, and humble yourself under his guidance. Find joy in what He is doing in your life, even if you don't understand it fully. He is the source of everything you need, both for this life and the next.

Don't let the world's troubles distract you or pull you away from focusing on him. The real challenge is to keep your focus on him, no matter what's happening around you. When Jesus is at the center of your thoughts, you can see things from his perspective.

Prayer

Lord Jesus, help me accept situations when things don't go my way. Prevent regret from turning into resentment. Remind me that you are in control and guide me to find joy in your plans. Keep me focused on you, seeing things from your perspective. Amen.

Day 42: Live Gratefully

Isaiah 6:3 (NIV)

And they were calling to one another: 'Holy, holy, holy is the Lord Almighty; the whole earth is full of his glory

Reflection

Jesus is inviting you to live a life of gratitude. He wants every moment of your life to be filled with thankfulness. The reason you can be grateful is because of his sovereignty. He is the Creator and Controller of the universe, and his glorious presence fills heaven and earth. When you criticize or complain, it's like you're saying you could run the world better than He can. From your limited human perspective, it might seem like He's not managing things well. But you don't know what He knows or see what He sees. If He showed you what goes on in heavenly realms, you would understand much more.

However, He's designed you to live by faith, not by sight. He lovingly shields you from knowing the future or seeing into the spiritual realm. Show your acknowledgment of his sovereignty by giving thanks in all circumstances.

Prayer

Heavenly Father, help me live a life of gratitude, recognizing your sovereignty over all. Guard me from criticism and complaints, and teach me to trust your wisdom and love. May I show my faith by giving thanks in all circumstances. Amen

Day 43: Do Not Worry About Tomorrow

Hebrews 3:13 (NIV)

But encourage one another daily, as long as it is called 'Today,' so that none of you may be hardened by sin's deceitfulness.

Reflection

Today is a gift from Jesus, so rejoice and be glad in it. Start the day with open hands of faith, ready to receive all that He has for you in this brief moment of your life. Be careful not to complain about anything, not even the weather, because He is the one orchestrating your circumstances.

The best way to handle things you don't like is to thank him for them. This act of faith frees you from resentment and allows him to work in the situation to bring about good. To find joy in today, you have to live within its limits. He divided time into 24-hour segments for a reason—He understands human weakness and knows you can only handle one day at a time. Don't worry about tomorrow or dwell on the past. There's abundant life to be found in his presence today.

Prayer

Heavenly Father, today is your gift. I embrace it with gratitude and faith. Help me avoid complaining and find joy in every circumstance. Guide me to live in the present moment, trusting in your provision. Amen.

Day 44: Forever the Same

Revelation 22:13 (NIV)

I am the Alpha and the Omega, the First and the Last, the Beginning and the End.

Reflection

In a world of constant changes, Jesus is the one who remains unchanged. He is the Alpha and the Omega, the First and the Last, the Beginning and the End. Find in him the stability you've been searching for. He created a perfectly ordered world that reflects his perfection. But now, the world is tainted by sin and evil. Everyone faces uncertainties. The only remedy to this threat is drawing closer to him. In his presence, you can confront uncertainty with perfect peace.

Prayer

Lord Jesus, in a world of constant changes, you are my unchanging stability. Help me draw closer to you, finding peace in your presence amidst uncertainty. Amen.

Day 45: Outside Your Comfort Zone

ISAIAH 12:2 (NIV)

Surely God is my salvation; I will trust and not be afraid. The Lord, the Lord himself, is my strength and my defense; he has become my salvation.

Reflection

Trust Jesus, and don't be afraid. Many things may feel out of control right now, and your routines may not be running smoothly. It's natural to feel more secure when life is predictable. Let him guide you to a place of stability that's higher than you and your circumstances. Take shelter under his wings, where you are completely secure. When you're shaken out of your comfort zone, hold onto his hand tightly and look for opportunities to grow. Instead of mourning the loss of your comfort, embrace the challenge of something new. He leads you from one level of glory to the next, preparing you for his kingdom. Say yes to the ways He works in your life. Trust him, and don't let fear hold you back.

Prayer

Heavenly Father, help me trust you and not be afraid when life feels out of control. Guide me to find stability in you and take shelter under your wings. When I'm shaken from my comfort zone, let me hold your hand

and embrace new challenges. Lead me from one level of glory to the next, preparing me for your kingdom. Amen.

Day 46: Anticipate Miracles

John 11:40 (NIV)

Then Jesus said, "Did I not tell you that if you believe, you will see the glory of God?"

Reflection

God's plan for your life is unfolding right in front of you. Sometimes the path you're on seems blocked, or it moves forward so slowly that you have to hold yourself back. Then, when the time is right, the way ahead suddenly clears—without you doing anything. What you've wanted and worked for is given to you freely, as a pure gift from him. You're amazed by how easily He works in the world, and you catch a glimpse of his power and glory.

Don't be afraid of your weaknesses because that's where his power and glory shine the brightest. As you keep going along the path He's set for you, relying on his strength to keep you going, expect to see miracles—and you will. Miracles aren't always obvious, but those who live by faith can see them clearly. Living by faith, instead of relying on what you can see, allows you to see his glory.

Prayer

Heavenly Father, I trust your unfolding plan for my life. Even in setbacks, I believe you'll clear the way effortlessly. Thank you for the pure gifts you provide, revealing your power and glory. Help me embrace weaknesses, knowing they reveal your strength. Guide me forward in faith, expecting miracles. Amen.

Day 47: Seeking Direction

Exodus 33:14 (NIV)

The LORD replied, "My Presence will go with you, and I will give you rest."

Reflection

Walk peacefully with Jesus through today. You might be worried about how you'll handle everything that's expected of you. Just take each step of the day one at a time, like you would on any other day. Instead of trying to figure out how you'll do everything, focus on being aware of his presence and on taking the next step. The busier your day is, the more help you can expect from him. This is a chance for you to learn because He made you to depend deeply on him, your Shepherd-King. Tough times wake you up and remind you that you need his help. When you don't know what to do, wait for him to show you the way. Trust that He knows what He's doing, and be ready to follow him. He'll give you strength, and He'll bless you with peace.

Prayer

Dear Lord Jesus, guide me peacefully through today. As I face my responsibilities, help me take each step with awareness of your presence. Remind me to rely on you, especially in busy times. Teach me to depend deeply on you, my Shepherd-King. In tough times, awaken me to my need for your help. When I'm unsure, show me the way, and grant me the strength and peace to follow you. Amen.

Day 48: The Path of Freedom

ROMANS 8:1-2 (NIV)

Therefore, there is now no condemnation for those who are in Christ Jesus, because through Christ Jesus the law of the Spirit who gives life has set you free from the law of sin and death.

Reflection

There is no condemnation for those who are connected to Jesus. The law of the Spirit of Life has freed you from the law of sin and death. But not many Christians understand how to live in this radical freedom that is their right. Jesus died to make you free, so live freely in him! To stay on the path of freedom, you need to keep your mind focused on him. Many voices say, "This is the way you should go," but only his voice tells you the true way.

If you follow the ways of the world, with all its attractions, you'll sink deeper and deeper into trouble. Even Christian voices can lead you astray, saying, "Do this!" "Don't do that!" "Pray like this!" "Don't pray like that!" If you listen to all those voices, you'll just get more confused. Instead, be like a simple sheep, listening for Jesus's voice and following him. He'll lead you to peaceful, green pastures and guide you along the right paths.

Prayer

Dear Lord Jesus, thank you for the freedom from condemnation. Help me stay focused on you to live freely. Guide me to discern your voice amidst others and lead me away from worldly influences. May I follow you to peaceful pastures. Amen.

Day 49: Break out of the Routine

PSALM 32:8 (NIV)

I will instruct you and teach you in the way you should go; I will counsel you with my loving eye on you.

Reflection

As you become more aware of Jesus's presence, you'll find it easier to figure out which way to go. This is one of the practical benefits of staying close to him. Instead of worrying about what's ahead or what you should do in the future, focus on staying connected with him. When you reach a point where you need to make a choice, He'll show you which way to go.

Many people are so focused on future plans and decisions that they miss the choices they need to make today. Without realizing it, they just go through the motions. Living like this can make life feel dull. They go through their days on autopilot, following the same old routines. But Jesus, the Creator of the universe, is incredibly creative. He won't let you keep going in the same old circles. Instead, He'll lead you on new adventures, showing you things you never knew. Stay connected with him. Follow his guiding presence.

Prayer

Dear Lord Jesus, help me stay aware of your presence each day. Guide my choices and lead me on new adventures with you. Amen.

Day 50: The Weight of Free Will

MATTHEW 6:33 (NIV)

But seek first his kingdom and his righteousness, and all these things will be given to you as well.

Reflection

Make pleasing Jesus your main goal as you go through today. Having this mindset will help you focus your energy instead of spreading it too thin. The free will He gave you comes with a big responsibility.

Every day, you face many choices. Some of these decisions you might ignore, making them by default. Without a clear focus to guide you, it's easy to lose your way. That's why it's so important to stay connected with him, being thankful for his presence in your life. You live in a broken world where things are always falling apart. Only a strong relationship with Jesus can keep you from falling apart too.

Prayer

Dear Lord, today I make pleasing you my main goal. Help me focus my energy and guide my choices. Keep me connected with you, thankful for your presence in my life. In this broken world, may our relationship keep me strong. Amen.

Day 51: Walk Confidently

2 CORINTHIANS 5:7 (NIV)

For we live by faith, not by sight.

Reflection

Walk by faith, not by what you can see. When you take steps of faith, relying on Jesus, you'll see what amazing things He can do for you. If you play it too safe in life, you'll never experience the excitement of seeing him work through you. When He gave you his Spirit, He gave you the power to live beyond your natural abilities and strength. So it's not right to measure your energy level against the challenges you face. The important thing isn't how strong you are, but how strong He is, and his strength is limitless. By staying close to him, you can accomplish his purposes with his strength.

Prayer

Dear Lord, help me walk by faith, not by sight. Guide me to take steps of faith, relying on you to work through me. Grant me the courage to experience the excitement of seeing you at work. Thank you for giving me your Spirit, empowering me to live beyond my natural abilities. May I rely on your limitless strength rather than my own. Amen.

Day 52: The Source of Strength

JOHN 14:16–17 (NIV)

And I will ask the Father, and he will give you another advocate to help you and be with you forever— the Spirit of truth. The world cannot accept him, because it neither sees him nor knows him. But you know him, for he lives with you and will be in you.

Reflection

The Lord, Creator of everything, the Lord of all that exists now and forever, chooses to live within you, filling you with his presence. Even though He is unimaginably vast, He dwells within someone so small. Be amazed by the power and glory of his Spirit within you! Even though the Holy Spirit is infinite, He's willing to help you. He's always ready to offer assistance—all you have to do is ask. When the path ahead seems easy and clear, you might be tempted to go it alone instead of relying on him. That's when you're most likely to stumble. Ask his Spirit to help you with each step you take. Don't overlook this amazing source of strength within you.

Prayer

Heavenly Father, Creator of all, I'm amazed by your presence within me. Thank you for dwelling in me despite my smallness. Help me to rely on your Spirit's assistance in all things. When the path seems easy, remind me to seek your guidance. Grant me the wisdom to never overlook the strength you provide within me. Amen.

Day 53: A Cheerful Heart

PROVERBS 17:22 (NIV)

A cheerful heart is good medicine, but a crushed spirit dries up the bones.

Reflection

Learn to laugh at yourself more often. Don't take everything so seriously, including yourself and your situation. Relax, knowing that Jesus is God and with you. When you prioritize his will above all else, life feels much less intimidating. Stop trying to control things that are his responsibility and beyond your reach. Embrace freedom by accepting the limits of what you can handle.

Laughter eases your burdens and lifts your spirit to heavenly realms. Your laughter reaches heaven and merges with the angels' songs of praise. Just as parents find joy in their children's laughter, He finds joy in hearing his children laugh. He is pleased when you trust him enough to live joyfully and lightheartedly.

Don't miss the Joy of his Presence by bearing the world's weight on your shoulders. Instead, take on his yoke and learn from him. his yoke is comfortable and pleasant; his burden is light and easy to carry.

Prayer

Dear Lord, help me to laugh at myself and not take life so seriously. Remind me that you are with me, and guide me to prioritize your will above all else. Teach me to let go of what I cannot control and embrace the freedom in my limitations. Let my laughter ease my burdens and bring joy to you. Help me trust you enough to live joyfully, taking on your light and easy yoke. Amen.

Day 54: My Love Endures Forever

JEREMIAH 31:3 (NIV)

The Lord appeared to us in the past, saying: "I have loved you with an everlasting love; I have drawn you with unfailing kindness.

Reflection

Jesus loves you with an everlasting love. It's hard for the human mind to grasp his constant affection. Your emotions may fluctuate with changing circumstances, and you might project your own feelings onto him. This can prevent you from fully experiencing his unwavering love. Instead, look beyond the ups and downs of life and realize that He's always gazing at you with love. Knowing that He's with you strengthens you as you receive and respond to his love. Remember, He is the same yesterday, today, and forever! Let his love flow into you continuously. Your need for him is as constant as his love pouring out to you.

Prayer

Dear Lord, thank you for your everlasting love. Help me to look beyond life's fluctuations and fully experience your unwavering affection. Strengthen me with the knowledge that you are always gazing at me with love. Let your love flow into me continuously, and remind me of your constancy. Amen.

Day 55: The Light of Hope

Psalm 40:2–3 (NIV)

He lifted me out of the slimy pit, out of the mud and mire; he set my feet on a rock and gave me a firm place to stand. He put a new song in my mouth, a hymn of praise to our God. Many will see and fear the Lord and put their trust in him.

Reflection

Self-pity is like a slimy, bottomless pit. Once you fall in, it's easy to sink deeper and deeper into despair. As you slide down those slippery walls, you're headed towards darkness and depression. Your only hope is to look up and see the light of Jesus's presence shining down on you. Even though it may seem faint from where you are, deep in the pit, those rays of hope can reach you no matter how far down you've gone.

When you focus on trusting him, you slowly rise out of the abyss of despair. Eventually, you can reach up and grab his hand. He'll pull you back into the light. He'll gently cleanse you, washing away the clinging despair. He'll cover you with his righteousness and walk with you along the path of life.

Prayer

Lord, help me to avoid self-pity, which leads to despair. When I feel myself sinking, remind me to look up and see your light shining down on me. Strengthen my trust in you, so I can rise out of despair and reach for your hand. Thank you for pulling me back into the light, cleansing me, and guiding me along the path of life. Amen.

Day 56: Feeling Disconnected from God

Genesis 28:15 (NIV)

I am with you and will watch over you wherever you go, and I will bring you back to this land. I will not leave you until I have done what I have promised you.

Reflection

Jesus is always with you and on your side, your constant companion and provider. The real question is whether you are with him and on his side. Even though He never leaves you, you can essentially "leave" him by ignoring him—thinking or acting as if He's not there. When you feel a distance in your relationship with him, you know where the problem lies. his love for you never changes; He is the same yesterday, today, and forever. It's you who change, like shifting sand, letting circumstances push you around. When you feel distant from him, whisper his name. This simple act, done in childlike faith, opens your heart to his presence. Speak to him with love and get ready to receive his love, which flows endlessly from the cross. He's delighted when you open yourself up to his loving presence.

Prayer

Lord, help me to always be with you and on your side. Forgive me when I ignore your presence and stray from your side. Thank you for your unchanging love, even when I am like shifting sand. When I feel distant from you, may I whisper your name in childlike faith, opening my heart to your presence. Fill me with your endless love flowing from the cross, and delight in my openness to your loving presence. Amen.

Day 57: Shun Excessive Planning

1 Peter 5:6–7 (NIV)

Humble yourselves, therefore, under God's mighty hand, that he may lift you up in due time. Cast all your anxiety on him because he cares for you.

Reflection

You won't find peace by over-planning and trying to control your future. This approach shows a lack of trust. When your mind is cluttered with various plans, peace might seem close but always slips away. No matter how much you prepare, unexpected events will disrupt your plans.

Your mind wasn't created to predict the future—it's not something you can do. Instead, God designed your mind for constant communication with him. Bring all your needs, hopes, and fears to him. Trust him with everything. Shift your focus from planning to finding peace.

Prayer

Lord, forgive me when I over-plan and try to control my future, showing a lack of trust in you. Help me understand that peace doesn't come from my own efforts, but from trusting in you. Teach me to bring all my needs, hopes, and fears to you, shifting my focus from planning to finding peace in constant communication with you. Amen.

Day 58: Finding Yourself

2 Corinthians 5:17 (NIV)

Therefore, if anyone is in Christ, the new creation has come: The old has gone, the new is here!

Reflection

I'm guiding you along a path that's just right for you. The closer you get to Jesus, the more you become your true self—the person He created you to be. Because you're unique, your journey with him is different from others'. But in his mysterious ways, He helps you walk this path while staying connected to others. In fact, the more you dedicate yourself to Jesus, the more freely you can love people.

Be amazed by the beauty of a life filled with his presence. Celebrate as you journey intimately together. Enjoy the adventure of discovering yourself by losing yourself in him.

Prayer

Lord, thank you for guiding me along the path that's just right for me. Help me to draw closer to you so that I may become my true self—the person you created me to be. As I journey with you, may I celebrate the beauty of a life filled with your presence and enjoy the adventure of discovering myself in you. Amen.

Day 59: Commit Solely to One Master

Matthew 6:24 (NIV)

No one can serve two masters. Either you will hate the one and love the other, or you will be devoted to the one and despise the other. You cannot serve both God and money.

Reflection

You can't serve two masters. If Jesus is truly your Master, you'll want to please him above everyone else. But if your goal is to please people, you'll become enslaved to them. People can be tough bosses when you give them that power over you.

If Jesus is the Master of your life, He'll also be your First Love. Your service to him is rooted in his vast, unconditional Love for you. The more you humble yourself before him, the more He'll lift you into a close relationship with him. The joy of being in his Presence surpasses all other pleasures. He wants you to shine with his joyful Light by growing closer to him.

Prayer

Lord, help me to serve you as my one true Master. May my desire to please you above all else guide my actions. Protect me from becoming enslaved to the expectations of others. Let my service to you be rooted in your unconditional love for me, and may humility draw me closer to you. In your presence, may I find joy that surpasses all other pleasures and shine with your light. Amen.

Day 60: A Peaceful Mind

Psalm 20:7 (NIV)

Some trust in chariots and some in horses, but we trust in the name of the Lord our God.

Reflection

Trust Jesus in all your thoughts. He knows that some thoughts are unconscious or semiconscious, and He does not hold you responsible for those. But you can direct conscious thoughts much more than you may realize. Practice thinking in certain ways—trusting him, thanking him—and those thoughts become more natural. Reject negative or sinful thoughts as soon as you become aware of them. Don't try to hide them from him; confess them and leave them with him.

Go on your way lightheartedly. This method of controlling your thoughts will keep your mind in his Presence and your feet on the path of Peace.

Prayer

Lord, help me to trust you in all my thoughts. Guide me to direct my conscious thoughts in ways that honor you—trusting and thanking you. When negative or sinful thoughts arise, empower me to reject them and confess them to you. May this practice keep my mind in your presence and lead me on the path of peace. Amen.

Conclusion

As you reach the end of this devotional, take a moment to reflect on the journey you've embarked upon over the past 60 days. This devotional was designed to accompany you through a transformative time in your life, offering spiritual nourishment and guidance as you step into the future. I hope these reflections and prayers have provided you with moments of peace, clarity, and a deeper connection with God.

Graduation is more than a ceremony; it's a significant milestone that marks the beginning of a new adventure. You have been equipped with knowledge, skills, and experiences that will serve you well in the years ahead. More importantly, you have had the opportunity to strengthen your faith and build a foundation rooted in God's love and wisdom. Remember that every challenge you face is an opportunity to grow, and every success is a testament to God's faithfulness in your life.

As you move forward, carry with you the lessons and insights you've gained from this devotional. Let them be a source of encouragement and inspiration in your daily life. Continue to seek God's presence, trust in his plans, and lean on his strength. Wherever your path leads, know that God is with you, guiding and supporting you every step of the way. May your journey be filled with abundant blessings, and may you always find peace and joy in his presence. Congratulations on your graduation, and may God bless you richly as you embark on this exciting new chapter.

Joanne Raines

Made in the USA
Middletown, DE
22 May 2024

54682000R00066